Step Wars

Jillian Powell

SERIES CONSULTANT: LORRAINE PETERSEN

NASEN House, 4/5 Amber Business Village, Amber Close, Amington,
Tamworth, Staffordshire B77 4RP

Rising Stars UK Ltd.
22 Grafton Street, London W1S 4EX
www.risingstars-uk.com

Text © Rising Stars UK Ltd.

The right of Jillian Powell to be identified as the author of
this work has been asserted by her in accordance with the
Copyright, Design and Patents Act 1998.

Published 2009

Cover design: Burville-Riley Partnership
Illustrator: Neil Smith
Text design and typesetting: Andy Wilson for Green Desert Ltd.
Publisher: Gill Budgell
Editor: Catherine Gilhooly
Series consultant: Lorraine Petersen

All rights reserved. No part of this publication may be reproduced, stored in a retrieval system, or transmitted in any form by any means, electronic, mechanical, photocopying, recording or otherwise without the prior permission of Rising Stars UK Ltd.

British Library Cataloguing in Publication Data.
A CIP record for this book is available from the British Library

ISBN 978-1-84680-500-4

Printed by Craft Print International Limited, Singapore

Contents

Characters	4
Scene 1: MOVING IN	7
Scene 2: THE BLUE LINE	16
Scene 3: A DECISION	27
Scene 4: WINNERS ALL ROUND?	36
In the chatroom ...	46

Characters

Jay
Jay's parents are divorced. His mum has married again and his new step-family is moving in. Worst of all, Jay has to share his room with his new step-brother, Conor.

Ross
Jay's best mate at school. Ross's parents are divorced too, and Ross is always on hand to give advice.

Conor
Conor is just as unhappy about things as Jay. Jay and Ross are football mad. Conor thinks football is boring. He likes music, drumming and being in a band.

Characters

Rashid
Conor's mate and fellow band member.

Amy
Jay's younger sister. She tries to help Jay and Conor get along. But Amy thinks Conor's band is cool, which really annoys Jay!

Narrator
The narrator tells the story.

Scene 1
MOVING IN

Narrator	Jay is on the phone to his best mate, Ross.

Ross What's up, mate?

Jay Today is the day.

Ross Oh. When?

Jay Any time now. I am *so* dreading it.

Ross You will get used to it. *I* did.

Jay No way. I can't forgive Mum for this.

Step Wars

Ross   She has to have a life
of her own you know.

Jay   Yeah, but she doesn't have to ruin ours!

Ross   I thought Amy was okay about it?

Jay   Yes, well, she gets to keep her room,
doesn't she? She isn't the one
who has to share with
a complete stranger.

Ross   Conor is not exactly a stranger.

Jay   Look, whose side are you on?

Ross   Yours, mate. Remember,
I have been there too!

Jay   Don't give me all that
happy step-family stuff!

Ross   I am just saying you *do* get used to it.
I did.

Scene 1 Moving in

Jay Well, I don't want to get used to it.
I want things the way they were,
just Mum, me and Amy.

Ross Well, that's not going to happen.
Not now your mum has married him.

Jay I hate it. I hate them! And most of all
I hate having to share my room
with that hippy Conor!

Narrator Conor is on his way to Jay's house.
He is on the phone to his best mate,
Rashid.

Conor I am *so* not looking forward to this.

Step Wars

Rashid It will be okay, you'll see.

Conor Why can't my parents stay together like yours?

Rashid Mine just row all the time.
I think they'd miss it!

Conor I don't want to move.

Rashid I thought it looked like a nice house.

Conor But it's not our house, is it?
Why can't we all live in Dad's house?
That way I'd get to keep my room.

Rashid I've told you. The grown-ups make the choices.
We just pick up the pieces!

Conor Well, it's not fair. I don't want to move.
And I really don't want to share a room with him.

Rashid That is a bit of a bummer, I agree.

Conor All he talks about is football.

Scene 1 Moving in

Rashid Bummer.

Conor He's got football posters all over the walls.

Rashid Double bummer!

Conor I mean, what have we got in common?

Rashid Um, you are family now I suppose. Well, step-family.

Conor Thanks, mate. You're a great help!

Narrator Conor and his dad arrive at Jay's house. Jay's mum and Amy are there to help them move in.

Amy Hi Conor. I'll help you move your stuff into your room.

Conor Don't you mean Jay's room?

Amy It's your room as well now!

Conor Does Jay see it like that?

Step Wars

Amy He'll have to. He can be a bit stubborn.
But he'll come round, you'll see.
What's that?

Conor It's my drum kit. Well, part of it.

Amy Wow! Are you a drummer? That's cool.

Conor Drums are great. I don't think about
anything else when I'm drumming.

Amy I'd love to hear you play.

Conor Oh, I am sure you will!
That is, if Jay lets me play them
in his room. I mean, in our room.

Amy Leave Jay to me. I'm used to him!

Narrator Amy shows Conor to the room
he will share with Jay.

Amy This is your room, Conor.
Conor and his dad are here, Jay.

Conor All right, Jay?

Scene 1 Moving in

Jay What's all that?

Conor It's just my clothes and stuff.

Jay No, I mean *that*.

Amy That's Conor's drum kit.
He plays the drums.
How cool is that?

Jay You can't play them in here.

Amy Don't listen to him, Conor.
I'll help you set them up
if you like.

Conor Rashid's going to bring
the rest of the kit later.
He plays the guitar.

Step Wars

Amy   Cool! What kind of stuff do you play?

Conor   Indie, mainly.

Amy   I love Indie.

Jay   Oi, you two!
            In case you haven't noticed,
            I'm trying to play a game here.

Narrator Conor looks over Jay's shoulder.

Conor   What level are you on?

Jay   Level five, why?

Conor   Oh, it's good that one.
            I got to level six last week.
            We can have a game together
            if you like.

Jay   No thanks. My mate Ross
            is coming round later.

Scene 1 Moving in

Conor Oh. Well, I suppose I had better get unpacked anyway.

Amy Did you clear some space for Conor, Jay?

Jay Why don't *you* clear some space Amy, since you two are such good mates?

Narrator Jay storms out. On the way, he kicks the drum kit. It sounds like thunder!

Scene 2

THE BLUE LINE

Narrator The next day, Conor has band practice. He gets back to find Jay has been up to something in their room.

Conor What's this?

Jay What does it look like?

Conor It looks like a blue line.

Jay You're not as stupid as you look.

Conor So what's it for?

Scene 2 The blue line

Jay Isn't it obvious? This is *my* side. That is *your* side.

Conor You *are* kidding?

Jay Do I look like I'm kidding?

Conor But that's crazy.

Jay You keep to your half, that's all I am saying.

Conor But I can't get to the TV!

Narrator Jay grabs the TV remote and puts it on the blue line.

Jay Sorted.

Conor What about the light switch? It's in your half!

Jay So you get a lamp your side. Easy.

Step Wars

Conor Mate, this is going too far.
Are you being serious?

Jay First off, I am being serious.
Secondly, I'm not your mate
or your brother. A week ago,
this was *my* room.

Conor Do you honestly think
I want to be your mate
or your brother? No way!
A week ago I had my own room too.

Jay Pity you didn't stay there.

Narrator Amy comes into the room.

Amy What's all the shouting about?

Conor Have you seen what your
stupid brother has done?

Scene 2   The blue line

Amy   Jay?

Jay   I've just marked out *my* bit and *his* bit. See?

Amy   Oh Jay!

Jay   Look, you can shut up.
You're not the one having to share.

Conor   Don't tell her to shut up!

Jay   She's my sister not yours.
I'll tell her to shut up if I want!

Amy   Just stop arguing!
It's like living in a war zone!

Jay   You said it. He's the invader!

Conor   I don't even want to be here!

Jay   Well, that's something we agree on.

Conor   It's not my fault your mum married my dad. We were doing fine before she came along!

Jay And we were doing fine too, weren't we, Amy?

Amy Don't drag me into it!

Jay We were fine.
Everything was fine before.

Conor Just how I feel.

Jay None of this mess is my fault.

Conor It's not my fault either, stupid!

Jay Don't call me stupid!

Narrator The doorbell rings.

Amy I'll go. You two sort yourselves out!

Narrator Amy goes to the door. It is Rashid with the rest of Conor's drum kit.

Amy Hello.

Rashid Hi. You must be Amy. I'm Rashid.

Scene 2 The blue line

Amy Conor's friend? You play the guitar, don't you?

Rashid He told you?

Amy I *so* want to hear your music.

Rashid Cool! Is Conor in?

Amy Yeah. He's upstairs.
I'm afraid my brother Jay
is being a bit stupid.

Rashid Step wars, huh?

Amy Something like that!

Rashid It'll work out. They just need to find something in common.
Is Jay into music?

Amy If you can call thrash metal, music!

Rashid Bummer!

Amy Are you and Conor into football?

Rashid Not really, only the big matches.

Amy Not much in common then.
Jay and his mates are football mad.

Rashid What about you, are you into music?

Amy I love music. I do a bit of singing.

Rashid Really? Nice one!

Narrator Amy helps Rashid carry the rest of Conor's drum kit up to the boys' bedroom. Jay and Conor aren't talking to each other.

Rashid Hi Conor.

Conor Hi Rash.

Rashid You must be Jay.

Scene 2 The blue line

Narrator Jay doesn't reply.

Amy Jay, I think Ross wants you.

Jay Ross is here?

Narrator Jay follows Amy downstairs.

Jay So where's Ross?

Amy I made that up to get you out of there. But I think Ross needs to talk some sense into you! You can't go on like this.

Jay Like what?

Amy These step wars! We all have to get along ... or at least try to.

Jay Why should we? We hardly know each other.

Amy Don't be stupid. We have to try, because we have to live together.

Step Wars

Jay But I don't want that.
I want things the way they were,
just you, me and Mum.

Amy You don't have to want it, Jay.
You just have to deal with it.

Jay I am dealing with it.

Amy By painting a blue line
down the middle of the bedroom?

Jay Exactly!

Scene 3

A DECISION

Narrator Conor is on the phone to Rashid.

Rashid So she can really sing?

Conor Amy is a brilliant singer.

Rashid Do you think she's up for singing in the band?

Conor I think so. She loves our stuff. I played her that CD we made.

Rashid Go on, ask her. If we want to enter this contest, we need a girl singer.

Conor I'll ask her. There's only one problem.

Rashid Jay?

Conor Got it in one.
Jay hates Amy even talking to me.

Rashid What is his problem?

Conor He thinks she's gone over to the enemy!

Rashid He needs to grow up!

Conor I know how he feels. We don't want
to be brothers, live in the same house
or share the same room.

Rashid Well, that's something you have
in common!

Conor Exactly, but he can't see it.

Rashid Well, we can't let Jay stand
in Amy's way. She'll make
a great lead singer.

Conor We don't have much time to practise.

Rashid I know. We need to get going!

Conor I'll ask Amy today. Jay can't stop her
being in the band.

Scene 3 A decision

Narrator Jay and Ross are on their way back from a football match.

Jay Did you see that goal? Slam! In the back of the net!

Ross It was a real banana!

Jay I just scooped it in!

Ross Looks like you scooped up half the pitch! Look at your kit. Your mum will go mad.

Jay Who cares? I've stopped worrying about Mum. She doesn't worry about me!

Ross That's not true. Your mum's great.

Jay *Was* great. Before she met *him*.

Ross Things are no better then?

Jay How can they be? My room isn't my own any more. And Conor's dad thinks he can ground me.

Ross   What did your mum say?

Jay   That's the worst bit. She sticks up
for him, against me. It's so unfair.

Ross   Yeah, well I've been there.
It does get better! With time.

Jay   You keep saying that!
But it's getting worse.

Ross   How?

Jay   It would be okay if Amy was on my side.

Ross   She's not?

Jay   (*mimics Amy*)
"Conor is so cool. Rashid is so cool.
They play in a band."
So they play in a band. So what?

Ross   Have you heard it, the band I mean?

Scene 3 A decision

Jay I've heard his drums!
I think he imagines he's beating his sticks on my head!

Ross Well, it sounds like a good way to get rid of anger! Anyway ... that goal, mate!
Bang in the back of the net!

Jay It was good, wasn't it?

Step Wars

Narrator Amy hears Jay and Ross come in.

Amy Hey guys.

Ross Hi Amy.

Amy Good match?

Ross Wicked! Jay got this amazing goal. He saw his chance and …

Amy Guess what?

Jay Mum and Jeff have split up and we've got our house back!

Amy Don't be stupid!

Jay Jeff has got it into his thick head that he is *not* my dad.

Amy Stop it, Jay. Conor and Rashid have asked me to join their band!

Jay *You?* In their band! What as?

Amy As the lead singer!

Scene 3 A decision

Ross Well, you are a good singer, Amy.

Jay Shut up Ross, whose side are you on?

Ross Well, no one's side. I was just saying ...

Jay Well don't.

Amy You can't stop me, Jay.

Jay I don't get it. Why are you doing this?

Amy Because I like their music and I want to be a singer.

Jay (*mimics Amy*)
"I like their music and I want to be a singer."
Get real, Amy. Conor is just doing this to get at *me*.

Step Wars

Amy   Oh, grow up! He's doing this
because they want to enter a contest.
They need a girl singer.

Jay   And it has to be you?

Amy   I want it to be me!
They want it to be me.
Conor heard me sing and ...

Ross   Nice one, Amy. I always thought ...

Jay   Shut up, Ross. He is just getting back
at me for the blue line.

Ross   Oh yeah. So how *is* that working
by the way?

Amy   It isn't. Jay has to cross the line
to get to his clothes.
Conor has to cross it to get out
of the room. How stupid is that?

Jay   But most of the time he knows
to stay on his side!

Amy   You can be so childish, Jay!

Scene 3   A decision

Jay And you are *so* grown up.
   A lead singer in a band!

Amy That's right. I'm a lead singer
   in Conor's band ... and if you
   don't like it, then I don't care.

Jay Fine! Come on Ross.
   Let's leave her to it.

Ross See you, Amy.
   (*whispers*) I think you'll be great.

Amy (*whispers*) Thanks, Ross.

Scene 4

Winners all round?

Narrator Jay and Ross are on the Internet.

Ross Any luck?

Jay Nothing.

Ross Try somewhere else.

Jay Where? We've tried everywhere.

Ross This is mad!

Jay Our team gets to the final and we can't get tickets!

Scene 4   Winners all round?

Ross   Well, we could.
We just can't afford them.

Jay   It's not fair.

Narrator   Amy comes in.

Amy   See you at the sports hall, guys.

Jay   What?

Amy   Ross knows where.

Jay   What are you talking about?

Ross   Um ... Amy is singing tonight.
I said we'd go.

Jay   You said what?

Ross   Come on, Jay. It might be fun.

Jay   Oh, my day just got better!
First we can't get tickets for the big match.
Now you want me to go to some
stupid band contest. No way!

Step Wars

Amy   Please, Jay.

Ross   Amy said there will be food and stuff.

Jay   What kind of mate are you, Ross?

Amy   Go on. Say you'll come.
Do it for me?

Ross   They might even win!

Jay   Great! So Conor's head
gets even bigger.

Ross   What's the prize, Amy?

Amy   The band gets played on local radio.

Jay   Big deal!

Amy   Oh, there is something else.
I forget what it is ...

Jay   Never mind. You won't win!

Ross   Don't be like that, Jay!
Amy is a great singer.

Jay   Well, *you* go then.

Scene 4   Winners all round?

Amy Please, Jay.

Jay All right. I give in. I will go, but only to see Conor's face when they say his band is rubbish!

Narrator The band practises all day.
Now the contest is about to begin.

Conor This is it, guys. Good luck everyone!

Rashid Good luck, Amy! Just enjoy it.

Amy I will. I just hope Jay and Ross have made it.

Narrator Amy peeps out to see.

Amy They came! Jay and Ross are right at the front, see?

Conor I hope Jay won't boo us!

Rashid Or throw eggs at us!

Step Wars

Narrator Jay and Ross are eating popcorn.

Jay How much longer?

Ross They're about to start. Hang on.

Jay I still think they're only doing this to get at me!

Narrator The contest begins. Conor's band is the last to play.

Amy Some of these other bands are really good!

Conor Don't panic! We're going to be the best, you'll see.

Rashid Come on, guys. It's our turn.

Narrator Conor's band plays their song. It goes really well and the crowd love it.

Ross Listen to that, Jay! They loved it. You must admit that they're good.

Scene 4 Winners all round?

Jay Must I?

Ross Oh, come on, Jay. They were great!

Jay Hmmm, I suppose they were okay.
Shush! What's happening?

Narrator The first results are in. Three bands have got to the final. Conor's band is one of them.

Ross There's Amy.
Let's say good luck.

Amy Isn't this amazing?

Ross You were great,
all of you.
Good luck in the final!

Jay Yeah, your band was okay.
You sang well, Amy. But it's no big deal,
is it? I mean, local radio.
It's hardly The X Factor!

Amy But that's not the only prize.
Didn't I say? The winner gets
five tickets for the big match.

Jay You're kidding?

Ross Amy, that's brilliant.
Go out there and win it!

Conor Are you coming, Amy?
We're on first. Jay, what did you think?

Jay (*after a long pause*) I think you did okay,
mate ... in fact, better than okay –
I think you can win this!

Ross Me too. So go for it!

Conor Thanks, guys.

Rashid Yes, thanks, guys.

Ross We'll be cheering all the way!

Scene 4 Winners all round?

Conor Really? That means a lot.

Jay Yes, really. We're right behind you!
We really want you to win,
don't we, Ross?

Ross We really, really do!

Amy Thanks! We'll try.

Narrator The band goes up to play.
Jay and Ross clap and cheer them.

Jay They're great, aren't they, Ross?

Ross Totally!

Step Wars

Jay   Do you think they will win?

Ross   Let's hope so! Five tickets for the final!

Narrator All the bands have played. It is time for the result. Conor's band has done it. They've won!

Conor   I can't believe it!

Rashid   Nor can I!

Amy   It's wicked!

Conor   We get to go on the radio!

Narrator The band get their prize. Then there's a party. Jay and Ross are first there.

Jay   (*slapping Conor on the back*) Brilliant, mate!

Conor   Thanks, Jay.

Scene 4 Winners all round?

Ross   We always knew you would win!

Rashid   Thanks, guys.

Conor   Hey, I was thinking.
You two are into football, aren't you?

Jay and Ross (*together*)
Just a bit.

Conor   Do you want to come to the big match?
We have five tickets. We can all go.

Amy   Thanks, Conor. That's really sweet.

Conor   So what do you say, guys?

Jay   The big match?
All five of us?
Thanks, Bro.

Rashid and Ross (*together*)
Looks like things just got better!

In the chatroom...

While you are surfing the net, you see this message written by Conor on a chatroom message board:

Message posted by
Conorlovesdrums

Tues 4.30 p.m.

I've just moved in with my dad's new wife. She's ok and so is her daughter but my new step-brother is a nightmare! ☹

He's just painted a line down the middle of our bedroom to keep us apart!

I think it's mad but how can I deal with him? Help! 😐

- Write a reply to Conor, offering him some good advice.

Role play ...

In your group, each choose a character from the play and create the following scene.

- Jay and Conor are arguing.
- Amy walks in and tries to make them be nice to one another.
- Ross and Rashid walk in. They also try to make things better.
- Remember to think about your body language as well as what you actually say.

Tip: The person who plays the narrator could observe the role play and give feedback on how well it worked.

In the hot seat ...

Choose one person to be Amy. Think back to Scene 3 where Amy tells Jay that she is in Conor's band. Everyone else asks Amy questions, e.g.

- *How did Jay's reaction make you feel?*
- *Did Ross's support help you?*
- *Will you stay in the band even if your brother is against it?*

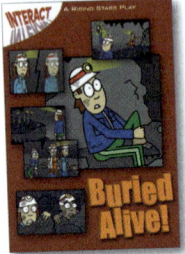

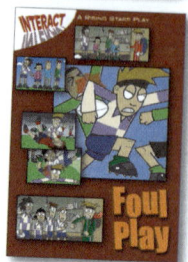

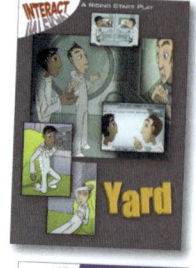

ASTRO-MAN
TOFFEE NOSE
BURIED ALIVE!
FOUL PLAY
PLANE CRAZY
YARD
DUMPED!
STEP WARS

Interact plays are available from booksellers or
www.risingstars-uk.com

For more information please call 0800 091 1602

RISING STARS